AF577372

BLACKS IN AMERICA

A PHOTOGRAPHIC RECORD

Robert A. Mayer

International Museum of Photography at George Eastman House, Rochester, New York.
Catalogue and exhibition supported by a special grant from the Eastman Kodak Company.

Acknowledgements:
I would like to express my appreciation to Museum staff members who assisted me in my research for and in preparation of this catalogue and exhibition: Carolee Aber, Sara Beckner, Amy Bellinger, Jim Conlin, Greg Drake, Andrew Eskind, Marianne Fulton, Michael Hager, Barbara Hall, Rick Hock, Susan Kramarsky, Ann McCabe, Gail McClain, Grant Romer, Barbara Schaeffer, Elizabeth Shepard, Rebecca Simmons, Rachel Stuhlman, James Via, David Wooters, Carolyn Zaft and Del Zogg. Susan Canton, Barbara Puorro Galasso and Sarah McDonald deserve very special thanks for the amount of work each contributed to preparation of the exhibition. Appreciation is also due the Eastman Kodak Company for a special grant which made this catalogue and the tour of the traveling version of the exhibition possible.

Robert A. Mayer

Exhibition at the International Museum of Photography at George Eastman House January 25 through March 30, 1986.

Photographs marked with an asterisk (*) are in the traveling version of the exhibition.

Library of Congress Catalogue Card Number 86-80319.
ISBN # 0-935398-12-0.

Permissions granted for reproduction of photographs or reprinting of texts:

Photographs:
Associated Press, Bruce Davidson, Roy DeCarava, Estate of Walker Evans, Ben Fernandez, Reed Hoffmann, David Hume Kennerly, Danny Lyon, Arnold Newman, Nicholas Nixon, Gordon Parks, Milton Rogovin, Estate of Arthur Rothstein, Aaron Siskind, Doris Ulmann by University of Oregon.

Texts:
Captain Joseph B. Anderson, Jr. from Bloods: An Oral History of the Vietnam War by Black Veterans, *edited by Wallace Terry. ©1984 Wallace Terry. Permission by Random House, Inc.*

James Baldwin from Notes of a Native Son *©1955, renewed 1983 James Baldwin. Permission by Beacon Press.*

Imamu Amiri Baraka (Le Roi Jones) from Black Poetry 1961-1967. *©1969 Le Roi Jones. Permission by The Sterling Lord Agency, Inc.*

Mary McLeod Bethune, Amanda Smith Jemand, Emma L. Shields, Mary Church Terrell and Sojourner Truth from Black Women in White America: A Documentary History, *edited by Gerda Lerner. ©1972 Gerda Lerner. Permission by Random House, Inc.*

Septima P. Clark from Echo in My Soul *with LeGette Blythe. ©1962 Septima Poinsetta Clark. Permission by E. P. Dutton & Co.*

Eldridge Cleaver from Soul on Ice. *©1968 Eldridge Cleaver. Permission by McGraw-Hill Book Company.*

Paul Laurence Dunbar from The Complete Poems of Paul Laurence Dunbar. *Permission by Dodd, Mead & Company, Inc.*

Langston Hughes from Selected Poems of Langston Hughes. *©1954 Langston Hughes. Permission by Alfred A. Knopf, Inc.*

Mahalia Jackson from Movin' on Up *with Evan McLeod Wylie. ©1966 Mahalia Jackson with Evan McLeod Wylie. Permission by E. P. Dutton & Co.*

James Weldon Johnson from Black Manhattan. *©1930 James Weldon Johnson, renewed 1958 Mrs. James Weldon Johnson. Permission by Charles Scribner's Sons.*

Martin Luther King, Jr., from Why We Can't Wait. *©1964 Martin Luther King, Jr. Permission by Harper & Row.*

Alice Walker from In Search of Our Mothers' Gardens. *©1983, 1973, 1970 Alice Walker. Permission by Harcourt Brace Jovanovich, Inc.*

Margaret Walker from Prophets for a New Day. *©1970 by Margaret Walker Alexander. Permission by Broadside Press.*

Booker T. Washington from Up from Slavery. *Permission by Doubleday & Co., Inc.*

Cover:
Doris Ulmann (Man and boy with boat) *ca. 1929-30. Gift of the 3M Co.*

"In the context of the Negro problem neither whites nor blacks, for excellent reasons of their own, have the faintest desire to look back; but I think the past is all that makes the present coherent, and further, that the past will remain horrible for exactly as long as we refuse to assess it honestly."[1]

In Notes of a Native Son, *James Baldwin wrote pointedly of the need to study the past to give meaning to the present. He also wrote in his book that "The story of the Negro in America is the story of America—or, more precisely, it is the story of Americans."*[2]

A special exhibition, organized by the International Museum of Photography at George Eastman House, looks at the past experience of Blacks in America through the photographic record that remains. This catalogue documents that exhibition: Blacks in America: A Photographic Record. *The photographs in the exhibition are drawn solely from the Eastman House collection; consequently, this photographic record is not complete. It does not detail the full spectrum of the history of Blacks in America, nor does it portray all of the leaders who made that historical record so rich and meaningful. Yet, it presents a moving story.*

In speaking of "the story of the Negro in America," James Baldwin also wrote that "it is not a very pretty story."[3] *There are instances in this catalogue when the photographic record supports that assessment in a vivid way. However, more of the photographs illustrate a positive "story of Americans"—portraits of important figures who helped forge American history, as well as many other Blacks, whose names we do not know, as they lived through their experiences from the mid-1800s to the present.*

Accompanying the photographs are quotations from the writings of numerous black authors. Nowhere is the story of Blacks in America told more movingly than in the books, poems or speeches of Blacks themselves. The tragedy of slavery, for example, can best be felt through the "narratives" of ex-slaves, such as in Frederick Douglass's autobiography, or in poetry, such as Frances E. W. Harper's "The Slave Auction." The meaning of the demonstrations of the 1960s comes most clear through Martin Luther King, Jr.'s statement that "The Negroes of America . . . shook off three hundred years of psychological slavery and said: 'We can make ourselves free'."[4]

Photography first came to America's shores in 1839, long after the savagery of slavery had been inflicted on America's Blacks.

The Eastman House collection has a number of photographs of Blacks taken in the 1850s and 1860s with the early daguerre-otype and ambrotype photographic processes (figures 1-7). It would appear from these photographs, by the style of dress, etc., that the "sitters" were free Blacks, most likely from the North and, probably, from the middle class, since photographers' fees, though minimal by today's standards, were not inexpensive in their time. An interesting series of photographs of Blacks from this period appears in the Studio Record Book maintained by Josiah Johnson Hawes who, with Albert Sands Southworth, operated one of the most famous American portrait studios in Boston. Among the small copy prints pasted in Hawes's Record Book are a number of black sitters. Three of these are of the same man, J. J. Johnson of Brattle Street (figure 8). Hawes's numbering system would indicate that Mr. Johnson visited the studio for a portrait session at least twice during September 1865.

The photographic record, presented through the images in this catalogue, also traces several recurring themes from the black experience. One of these is the importance of religion. It is fitting that one of the earliest images is a daguerreotype of a minister (figure 1).

1. Unidentified photographer, *(Unidentified minister)*, ca. 1850s.

2. Unidentified photographer, *(Unidentified woman)*, ca. 1850s.
Gift of Eaton Lothrop

3. Unidentified photographer, *(Unidentified man)*, ca. 1850s.

5. Unidentified photographer, *(Unidentified woman)*, ca. 1860s.
Gift of Eaton Lothrop

4. Unidentified photographer, *(Three men)*, ca. 1860s.

6. Williams, *(Unidentified woman)*, ca. 1860s.
Gift of Eaton Lothrop

7. Unidentified photographer, *(Unidentified man)*, ca. 1860s.

8. Josiah Johnson Hawes, *J.J. Johnson (3 views)*, from Hawes's Studio Record Book, ca. September, 1865.
Gift of Alden Scott Boyer

SLAVERY, THE CIVIL WAR AND EMANCIPATION

In the very important Civil War photographic document Gardner's Photographic Sketchbook of the War, *the inhumaneness of slavery can be sensed in William R. Pywell's photograph of an empty slave pen in Alexandria, Virginia, taken in August 1862 (figure 9). One can envision it as it had been, crowded with men, women and children "defenseless in their wretchedness,"[5] each to be sold, as Frederick Douglass wrote, "like a beast in the market."[6]*

Two of the other recurring themes developed through the photographs in this exhibition trace back to these early days: the drive for education and the patriotic service of Blacks in the nation's armed forces.

A group of photographs show slave children who were released by Union troops. Two of these show a brother and sister who were freed from their owner, Thomas White of Mathews County, Virginia, by Captain Riley of the 6th U.S.O.I. on February 20, 1864, and taken to the Society of Friends in Philadelphia to be educated at the Orphan's Shelter (figures 10-11). The cartes-de-visite were sold to raise funds to educate the children. The captions on the photographs explain that the children's mother had been "beaten, branded and sold at auction because she was kind to Union Soldiers." She had been taken away to be sold in Richmond only seven days before the children were freed. Their story, when placed next to the Pywell photograph, puts the pain of the slave market into chilling perspective.

The other pair of photographs show four slave children who were freed and brought North by abolitionists to emphasize the plight of slaves (figures 12-13). The proceeds from sale of the photographs were to be used to educate freed slaves who had come under the jurisdiction of the Union Army in the New Orleans area. A caption on one of these photographs points out that the children had been turned out of a hotel in Philadelphia because of their "color." This comment was a telling statement about racist attitudes in the North regardless of abolitionist sentiment and the war itself.

Three photographs, two in stereo form, relate to the service of Blacks with the Union Army. One of the stereo views, "A group of 'Contrabands'," shows several runaway slaves who joined the Union troops (figure 14). The name "Contrabands" was given to these runaways by Union General Benjamin Butler. A caption on the back of this photograph, written a quarter century after it was taken, said that "these Negroes were employed by the Government as teamsters, laborers, etc." Another image from Gardner's Photographic Sketchbook of the War *shows a group of Blacks on one of the more grisly labor details: It is called "Burial Party, Cold Harbor, Virginia" and was taken in April 1865 (figure 15).*

The other stereo view, taken by Alexander Gardner himself, shows "A Wounded Negro, Culpepper (Virginia)" (figure 16). Made in 1862, it is one of the earliest such pictures produced.

The final photograph in the section relating to emancipation starts the thread throughout the exhibition of the struggle for civil rights. It is a portrait of Sojourner Truth, the ex-slave who took her special name and crisscrossed the country speaking out for the freedom of her people (figure 17). In 1867, at a Convention of the Equal Rights Association, prior to the passage of the 14th Amendment to the United States Constitution, this valiant woman spoke not only for her race but also for her sex: "There is a great stir about colored men getting their rights, but not a word about the colored women; and if colored men get their rights, and not colored women theirs, you see the colored men will be masters over the women, and it will be just as bad as it was before."[7] On the carte-de-visite portrait of Sojourner Truth there appears the phrase "I Sell the Shadow to Support the Substance." This refers to her need to sell copies of her photographs to raise funds with which to live.

THE SLAVE AUCTION

The sale began—young girls were there,
  Defenseless in their wretchedness,
Whose stifled sobs of deep despair
  Revealed their anguish and distress.

The mothers stood with streaming eyes,
  And saw their dearest children sold;
Unheeded rose their bitter cries,
  While tyrants bartered them for gold.

And woman, with her love and truth—
  For these in sable forms may dwell—
Gaz'd on the husband of her youth,
  With anguish none may paint or tell.

And men, whose sole crime was their hue,
  The impress of their Maker's hand,
And frail and shrinking children, too,
  Were gathered in that mournful band.

Ye who have laid your love to rest,
  And wept above their lifeless clay,
Know not the anguish of that breast,
  Whose lov'd are rudely torn away.

Ye may not know how desolate
  Are bosoms rudely forced to part,
And how a dull and heavy weight
  Will press the life-drops from the heart

Frances E. W. Harper *(1825-1911)*

The grim horrors of slavery rise in all their ghastly terror before me; the wails of millions pierce my heart and chill my blood. I remember the chain, the gag, the bloody whip; the death-like gloom overshadowing the broken spirit of the fettered bondman; the appalling liability of his being torn away from wife and children, and sold like a beast in the market.

Frederick Douglass *from a letter "To My Old Master, Thomas Auld." (1848)*

9. William R. Pywell, *Slave Pen, Alexandria, Virginia*, August 1862.*

Slavery does away with fathers, as it does away with families . . . (My mother and I) were separated, according to the common custom, when I was but an infant, and, of course, before I knew my mother from anyone else . . . There is not, beneath the sky, an enemy to filial affection so destructive as slavery. It has made my brothers and sisters strangers to me; it converted the mother that bore me, into a myth; it shrouded my father in mystery, and left me without an intelligible beginning in the world.

Frederick Douglass *from*
My Bondage and My Freedom
(1855)

10. P.F. Cooper, *As We Found Them*, 1864.*

11. P.F. Cooper, *As They Are Now*, 1864.*

12. M.H. Kimbell, *Rebecca, Augusta and Rosa*, 1863.*

13. J. McClees, *These Children*, 1863.
Gift of the Eastman Kodak Co.*

14. Taylor and Huntington, *A group of "Contrabands,"* ca. 1863.* Detail of stereo.

No sooner had the armies, East and West, penetrated Virginia and Tennessee than fugitive slaves appeared within their lines. They came at night, when the flickering camp-fires shone like vast unsteady stars along the black horizon: old men and thin, with gray and tufted hair; women, with frightened eyes, dragging whimpering hungry children; men and girls, stalwart and gaunt,—a horde of starving vagabonds, homeless, helpless, and pitiable, in their dark distress.

William E. B. DuBois *from*
The Souls of Black Folk
(1903)

15. John Reekie, *Burial Party, Cold Harbor, Virginia,* April 1865.*

16. Alexander Gardner, *A Wounded Negro, Culpepper,* 1862. Gift of Albert Turner.* Detail of stereo.

17. Randall, *Sojourner Truth,* ca. 1860s.*

BLACKS IN THE NORTH: THE END OF THE CENTURY

A series of photographs, reminiscent of the several early portraits, dominate the next section of the exhibition (figures 18-23). They are all drawn from cities in the north or the midwest and, with the exception of one, are of unidentified men and women. In photographic terms, they are albumen prints in either carte-de-visite or cabinet card formats or tintypes. They span the decades between the 1860s and 1890s. Those for which the photographer's studio is known are from Hartford, Connecticut, Troy, New York, and Alliance, Ohio. The identified portrait is Fred S. Philips of Salem, New Jersey, taken by Pach Brothers, a prominent New York City studio.

As in the earlier daguerreotypes and ambrotypes, the sitters appear well-dressed and at ease posing in the photographer's studio.

An interesting pair of photographs are gem tintypes, each of an unidentified black man that appears in a white family album. Apparently these young men were servants and were photographed for the albums as part of the family group (figures 24-25).

Another photographic album in the Museum's collection shows all of the members of the Massachusetts House of Representatives in 1873. L. Hayden of Boston appears as the only Black among the State's elected officials portrayed in the album (figure 26).

Several other photographs are chronologically part of this period but form part of the themes that run through the exhibition. "U.S. Overland Stage," taken around 1867, shows a stage coach on the Kansas to California route. All of the soldiers who are riding as protection are Black (figure 27).

Three other pictures begin the recurring theme related to legal systems and justice. One is a carte-de-visite portrait of a "prison baby" (Willis D. Mason, born November 6, 1875). It was taken by Z. Gilbert of Joliet, Illinois, and appears to be of a child born to a woman held in prison (figure 28). A second is entitled "Whipping Post, Delaware." Taken by Samuel M. Fox, it shows a black man tied to a post with another man preparing to flog him. It dates to 1889 (figure 29). The third photograph is one of the most disturbing pictures in the exhibition. Taken by William H. Vander Weyde in the 1890s at Sing Sing Prison in Ossining, New York, it shows a man being strapped into an electric chair. We know nothing about the circumstances of the situation—the crime, the trial, the prisoner's name. The power of the picture speaks for itself (figure 30).

18. Prescott and White, *(Unidentified woman)*, ca. 1860s.
Gift of Alden Scott Boyer*

19. Schoonmaker, *(Unidentified man)*, ca. 1860s.
Gift of Alden Scott Boyer*

20. Unidentified photographer, *(Unidentified woman)*, 1879.*

21. Unidentified photographer, *(Unidentified man)*, ca. 1880s. Gift of H.A. Beauchamp*

22. Pach Brothers, *Fred S. Philips, Salem, New Jersey*, ca. 1880s.*

24. Unidentified photographer, *(Unidentified man)* in album, ca. 1860s. Gift of 3M Co.

23. Lorin E. Miller, *(Unidentified woman)*, ca. 1880s.
Gift of 3M Co.*

25. Unidentified photographer, *(Unidentified man)* in album, ca. 1860s.

26. Unidentified photographer, *L. Hayden, Boston (Member of the Massachusetts House of Representatives)*, 1873.

27. Alexander Gardner, *U.S. Overland Stage*, ca. 1867.*

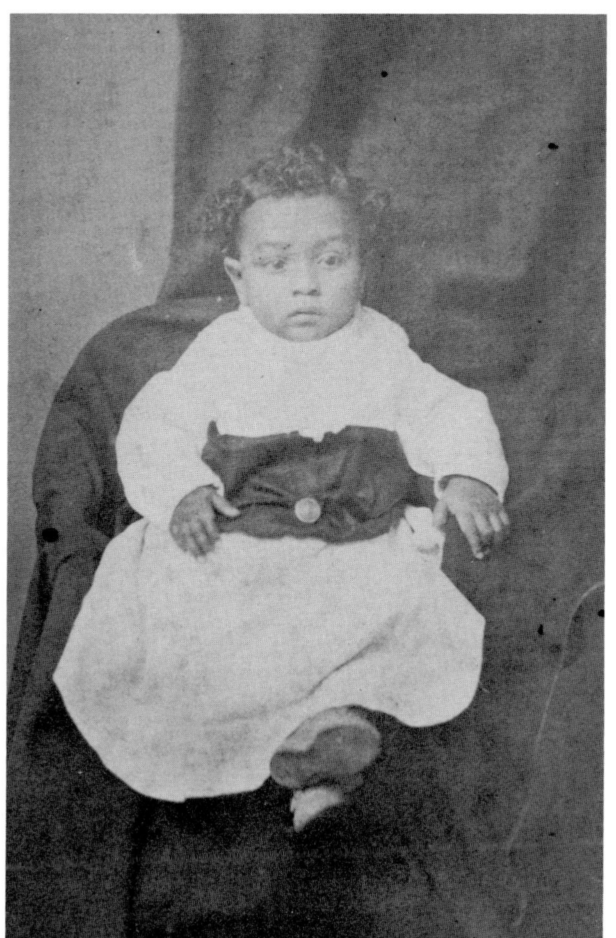

28. Z. Gilbert, *(Prison Baby)*, ca. 1876.
Gift of Alden Scott Boyer

29. Samuel M. Fox, *Whipping Post, Delaware*, ca. 1889.
Gift of 3M Co.

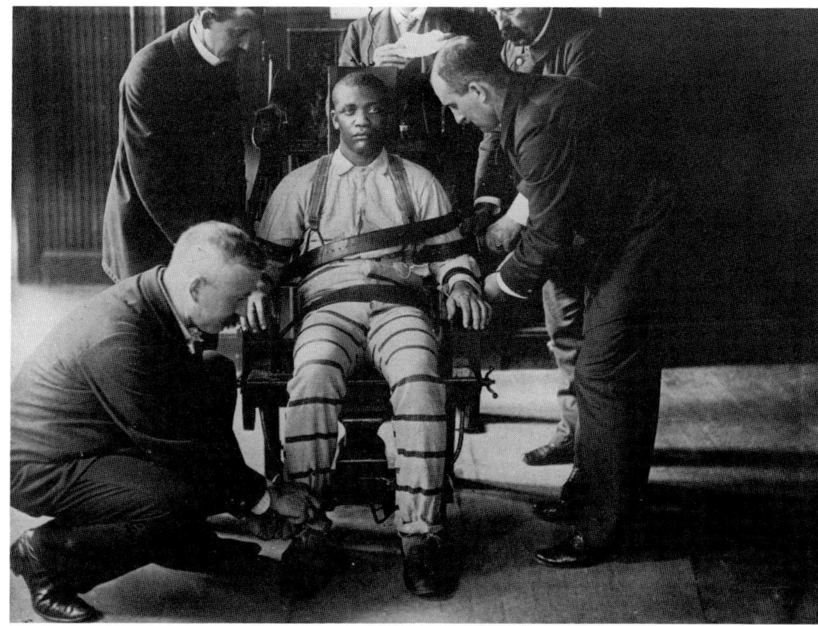

30. William Vander Weyde *(Sing Sing Prison)*, ca. 1890s.

For this much all men know: despite compromise, war, and struggle, the Negro is not free. In the backwoods of the Gulf States, for miles and miles, he may not leave the plantation of his birth; in well-nigh the whole rural South the black farmers are peons, bound by law and custom to an economic slavery, from which the only escape is death or the penitentiary.

William E. B. DuBois *from*
The Souls of Black Folk
(1903)

Covering a span of sixty years, over thirty photographs show various aspects of the lives of Blacks primarily in the rural South. As Amanda Smith Jemand wrote in 1901: "The Southerner boasts this is a white man's country. I deny it; it is my country as well as his. The South, especially, is as much the black man's as the white man's; for every plantation, town and city shows the work of his hand."[8] William E. B. DuBois, two years later, wrote that "in well-nigh the whole rural South the black farmers are peons, bound by law and custom to an economic slavery, from which the only escape is death or the penitentiary."[9]

The first photograph in this section of the exhibition is a stereograph, the title of which reads "Cotton is King, Plantation Scene, Georgia, U.S.A." (figure 31). It shows field hands picking cotton, one of them a young girl. Completing the series on King Cotton are two other stereo views, one of a group of men and boys waiting for their wagon teams at a cotton gin in Florida, the other showing bales of cotton being loaded on a levee in Texas (figures 32-33). The three photographs span the twenty year period from 1879 to about 1900. However, they clearly illustrate life for many Southern Blacks as it continued well into the 20th century. For even in the 1960s, educator Septima P. Clark would recall in her autobiography that her pupils "didn't come in until the cotton had been picked, and often it was Christmas and sometimes even January before all the cotton was gleaned."[10]

Showing other aspects of life in the South for Blacks at the end of the 19th century are three additional stereographs. One shows a group, including a number of Blacks, celebrating Inauguration Day in Washington, D.C. on March 4, 1889 (figure 34). Another depicts a family group in St. Augustine, Florida, and the third shows women at a washing camp in South Carolina (figures 35-36).

The post Civil War years led to extensive efforts by many people to try to provide educational opportunities to the freed Blacks. Four pictures from the end of the 19th century expand this theme. Three stereographs show "The Colored School" in Vicksburg, Mississippi, the "Stanton Institute" in Jacksonville, Florida, and the "Jubilee Singers" from Fisk University, Nashville, Tennessee (figures 37-39). These three pictures document the effort to offer education at all levels. The fourth photograph is a portrait of Booker T. Washington, the founder of Tuskegee Institute (figure 40). In his autobiography, Up From Slavery, *Washington pointed out what an outstanding accomplishment these efforts were since "only sixteen years before (the laying of a cornerstone at Tuskegee in 1882)... no Negro could be taught from books without the teacher receiving the condemnation of the law or of public sentiment..."[11]*

The final picture from the 19th century directly related to Southern life is a group picture entitled "Union of the Races" taken in Jacksonville, Florida, and shows black and white men and women gathered on a porch together (figure 41).

The 19th century closed with the United States emerging as a world power as a result of the Spanish American War. Booker T. Washington, in addressing a meeting in Boston at the end of the War, said:

"When you have gotten the full story of the heroic conduct of the Negro in the Spanish-American War, have heard it from the lips of Northern soldier and Southern soldier, from ex-abolitionist and ex-masters, then decide within yourselves whether a race that is thus willing to die for its country should not be given the highest opportunity to live for its country."[12]

Recognizing this contribution to the War, the "9th Ohio (colored)" troop was depicted in a stereograph taken at Camp Alger in Virginia, a detail of which is reproduced in this catalogue (figure 42).

31. Strohmeyer and Wyman, *Cotton is King, Plantation Scene (Georgia)*, 1895.*

32. Kilburn Brothers, *Waiting for your team at the cotton gin (Florida)*, 1879.*

33. Keystone View Co., *Cars loaded with cotton bales on levee (Texas)*, ca. 1900. Gift of Sister M. Rosalina*

Although it is the capital of the United States, Washington, D.C. has been primarily a "Southern" city. It has always housed many Blacks but, as with the rest of the South, it has not always been hospitable to this population. In 1907 Mary Church Terrell wrote that "surely nowhere in the world do oppression and persecution based solely on color of the skin appear more hateful and hideous than in the capital of the United States..."[13]

Two photographs from Washington, D.C. in the first decade of the 20th century sum up the sad facts of Mrs. Terrell's comments. One shows the shattered back yards of a slum area, a lone black woman leaning on her porch railing (figure 43). The other is a picture of a tiny girl sitting in a chair in front of a curtain-draped window. Hanging precariously in the window frame is a sign for the "Temporary Home for Colored Children" (figure 44).

Both of these photographs were taken by Lewis W. Hine. Noted for his famous images of immigrants arriving at Ellis Island and children working in factories and mines, Hine took an eloquent series of photographs of black life in the South between the turn of the century and the early 1930s. A number of these highlight the section of the exhibition dealing with the rural South (figures 45-47 and 50-55).

Among the Southern Blacks depicted by Hine, we see families or individuals at home in shacks, as well as in finely appointed houses or, as in one instance, a public library. We see two women hard at work, one in a print shop, the other in a tobacco factory.

We also find the continuing theme of education with a pair of photographs of a group of little children being cared for in a nursery school and two men attending a literacy class.

In the middle of this series is a Hine portrait of a sergeant at the Rainbow Division Camp, taken in 1917 during America's participation in World War I (figure 48). A stereograph, published by the Keystone View Company, shows an enthusiastic New York City crowd welcoming the "Colored Veterans of the 15th Regiment, 369th Infantry" on their return from fighting in Europe (figure 49). When America went to war, Blacks were again there doing their share.

Doris Ulmann, a wealthy white woman from the North, had taken up photography and focused her lens primarily upon the people of the South. In doing so, she produced a rich body of work portraying black life in South Carolina in the 1929-30 period. Four of Ulmann's images appear in the exhibition (figures 56-59). All continue the exhibition's sub-themes. One shows a crowded church service filled with joyous women in summer white dresses. Another shows a group of men on a work detail, all dressed in striped prison uniforms. The other two depict the work ethic with which the black experience is imbued, seen also in the earlier series by Lewis Hine.

Natural disasters and the economic plight of the Great Depression were the reasons that the final group of photographs from the rural South were produced. Lewis Hine documented an American Red Cross relief effort for drought sufferers in Mississippi in 1930. The photograph from this series displayed in the exhibition shows a distribution center for seeds to be given to stricken farmers (figure 60). A group of white farmers, all of whom have received their packages, stand on one side of the porch. A long line of black farmers wait in line to receive their packages on the other side of the porch.

The Farm Security Administration's team of photographers captured images of the plight of Blacks in the rural South, as well as of whites and migrant workers across the country. Walker Evans, Dorothea Lange and Arthur Rothstein all produced strong photographs from this period (figures 61-64).

34. Kilburn Brothers, *Hurrah, Inauguration Day (Washington, D.C.)*, March 4, 1889.

35. George Barker, *A family group, St. Augustine, Florida*, 1888.

36. J.A. Palmer, *Washing Camp (South Carolina)*, ca. 1870s.

37. Kilburn Brothers, *The Colored School, Vicksburg (Mississippi)*, 1891.*

38. Unidentified photographer, *Stanton Institute, Jacksonville (Florida)*, ca. 1890s.*

39. Black, *Jubilee Singers, Fisk University, Nashville, (Tennessee)*, ca. 1870s-1880s.*

I was born a slave on a plantation in Franklin County, Virginia. I am not quite sure of the exact place or exact date of my birth . . . I was born in a typical log cabin, about fourteen by sixteen feet square. In this cabin I lived with my mother and a brother and sister after the Civil War, when we were all declared free . . .

During the whole of the Reconstruction period our people throughout the South looked to the Federal government for everything, very much as a child looks to its mother. This was not unnatural. The central government gave their freedom, and the whole nation had been enriched for more than two centuries by the labour of the Negro . . .

. . . it was hard for me to realize that I was to be honoured by a degree from the oldest and most renowned university in America . . . My whole former life—my life as a slave on a plantation, my work in the coal mine, the times when I was without food and clothing, when I made my bed under a sidewalk, my struggles for an education, the trying days I had had at Tuskegee, days when I did not know where to turn for a dollar to continue the work there, the ostracism and sometimes oppression of my race—all this passed before me and nearly overcame me.

I think that the whole future of my race hinges on the question as to whether or not it can make itself of such indispensable value that the people in the town and state where we reside will feel that our presence is necessary to the happiness and well-being of the community.

Booker T. Washington *from*
Up from Slavery
(1901)

40. Unidentified photographer, *Booker T. Washington*, ca. 1900. Gift of 3M Co.*

41. A.D. White, *Union of the Races, Jacksonville (Florida)*, ca. 1890s. Gift of Alden Scott Boyer.

42. Charles Webster and Josephus Albee, *9th Ohio (colored) at Camp Alger, Virginia*, ca. 1897. Gift of 3M Co. Detail of stereograph by Barbara Puorro Galasso*

Surely nowhere in the world do oppression and persecution based solely on the color of the skin appear more hateful and hideous than in the capital of the United States, because the chasm between the principles upon which this government was founded, in which it still professes to believe, and those which are daily practiced under the protection of the flag, yawn so wide and deep.

Mary Church Terrell *from "What It Means to Be Colored in the Capital of the United States" (January 1907)*

43. Lewis W. Hine, *(Slums in Washington, D.C.)*, 1908. Gift of the Photo League of N.Y.*

44. Lewis W. Hine *(Orphan)*, ca. 1906. Gift of the Photo League of N.Y.*

45. Lewis W. Hine, *(Mother and two children)*, ca. 1910s. Gift of the Photo League of N.Y.*

46. Lewis W. Hine, *(Unidentified woman)*, ca. 1910.
Gift of the Photo League of N.Y.*

They had very dark skin. My grandmother was low and fat, she had long hair and would have it braided all over her head. She wore her dresses very long and an apron as long as her dress. My grandfather was tall with long beards under his chin. His hair was very long. They lived on their own little farm and never had what I called a "hard time," they raised corn, cotton and vegetables, cured their own meat and made syrup from cane. They had eight children, six boys and two girls. My father said they would whip them if they wouldn't mind them, or any grown person.

Mrs. G. S. *as quoted by* **Alice Walker** *in "But Yet and Still the Cotton Gin Kept on Working..." (1970) from* In Search of Our Mothers' Gardens *(1983)*

47. Lewis W. Hine, *(Unidentified man)*, ca. 1915.
Gift of the Photo League of N.Y.*

48. Lewis W. Hine, *(Sergeant) Rainbow Division Camp*, 1917.
Gift of the Photo League of N.Y.*

49. Keystone View Co., *Colored Veterans of the 15th Regiment 369th Infantry Marching up Fifth Avenue, N.Y.C.*, 1918.*

50. Lewis W. Hine, *(Children in nursery school)*, ca. 1920.
Gift of the Photo League of N.Y.*

51. Lewis W. Hine, *(Literacy class)*, ca. 1920.
Gift of the Photo League of N.Y.*

52. Lewis W. Hine, *(Linotyper)*, ca. 1920.
Gift of the Photo League of N.Y.

53. Lewis W. Hine, *(Tobacco worker)*, ca. 1920.
Gift of the Photo League of N.Y.

Tens of thousands of Negro women in the South are employed ten hours daily in old, unclean, malodorous buildings in which they are denied the most ordinary comforts of life. Either standing all day, in some occupations, or, in others, seated on makeshift stools or boxes with no back support, they toil incessantly throughout the long tedious hours of the work day, except for a half-hour lunch period at noon.

Emma L. Shields *from "Negro Women and the Tobacco Industry" (1921)*

54. Lewis W. Hine, *(Women at home)*, ca. 1920.
Gift of the Photo League of N.Y.

55. Lewis W. Hine, *(Men in library)*, ca. 1920.
Gift of the Photo League of N.Y.

56. Doris Ulmann, *(Church meeting)*, ca. 1929-30.*

57. Doris Ulmann, *(Chain Gang)*, ca. 1929-30.
Gift of 3M Co.*

58. Doris Ulmann, *(Woman plowing)*, ca. 1929-30.
Gift of 3M Co.

59. Doris Ulmann, *(Man and boy with boat)*, ca. 1929-30.
Gift of 3M Co.*

60. Lewis W. Hine, *Red Cross delivering seeds to drought sufferers (Mississippi)*, 1930.
Gift of the Photo League of N.Y.*

61. Walker Evans, *Vicksburg, Mississippi*, 1936.*

62. Dorothea Lange, *Ex-Slave with a Long Memory, Alabama*, 1937.*

63. Arthur Rothstein, *One Family, Alabama*, 1938.
Gift of Arthur Rothstein*

64. Arthur Rothstein, *Gee's Bend, Alabama*, 1938.
Gift of Arthur Rothstein

Among the many black leaders that emerged during the first decades of the 20th century, there were noted individuals in the arts and education. Nickolas Muray, a prominent celebrity portrait photographer of the 1920s to the 1960s, took a striking picture of poet Langston Hughes around 1925 (figure 65). Edward Steichen did a series of photographs of Paul Robeson a decade later (figure 66). And Aaron Siskind produced an historic moment when Mary McLeod Bethune, the famous educator, stood on the altar of a church with union leader A. Philip Randolph at a service for pullman porters in the mid 1930s (figure 67).

66. Edward Steichen, *Paul Robeson*, ca. 1935.
Bequest of the Estate of Edward Steichen by direction of Joanna T. Steichen*

65. Nickolas Muray, *Langston Hughes*, ca. 1925.
Gift of the Muray family*

THE NEGRO SPEAKS OF RIVERS

I've known rivers:
I've known rivers ancient as the world and older than the flow of human blood in human veins.

My soul has grown deep like the rivers.

I bathed in the Euphrates when dawns were young.
I built my hut near the Congo and it lulled me to sleep.
I looked upon the Nile and raised the pyramids above it.
I heard the singing of the Mississippi when Abe Lincoln went down to New Orleans, and I've seen its muddy bosom turn all golden in the sunset.

I've known rivers:
Ancient, dusky rivers.

My soul has grown deep like the rivers.

Langston Hughes
(1902-1966)

My mother, father, and older brothers and sisters had been slaves until the Emancipation Proclamation . . .

Mother was of royal African blood, of a tribe ruled by matriarchs . . .

On October 3, 1904, I opened the doors of my school, with an enrollment of five little girls, aged from eight to twelve, whose parents paid me fifty cents weekly tuition. My own child was the only boy in the school. Though I hadn't a penny left, I considered cash money as the smallest part of my resources. I had faith in a living God, faith in myself, and a desire to serve . . .

Near by was a field, popularly called Hell's Hole, which was used as a dumping ground. I approached the owner, determined to buy it. The price was $250. In a daze, he finally agreed to take five dollars down, and the balance in two years. I promised to be back in a few days with the initial payment. He never knew it, but I didn't have five dollars. I raised this sum selling ice cream and sweet-potato pies to the workmen on construction jobs, and I took the owner his money in small change wrapped in my handkerchief. That's how the Bethune-Cookman College campus started . . .

For I am my mother's daughter, and the drums of Africa still beat in my heart. They will not let me rest while there is a single Negro boy or girl without a chance to prove his worth.

Mary McLeod Bethune *from "Faith That Moved A Dump Heap" (June 1941)*

67. Aaron Siskind, *(Mary McLeod Bethune and A. Philip Randolph)*, ca. 1935. Gift of Aaron Siskind*

Poet-playwright-diplomat James Weldon Johnson called Harlem a Negro metropolis in his book Black Manhattan.[14] *He talked of the struggle of its residents to make a living, the power of its churches, its disintegrating forces, and its gaiety and zest for life.*

Around 1939 a group of members of the Photo League of New York took an extensive series of photographs, which they formed into an exhibition called "Harlem Document." Fifteen of these photographs by different members of the Photo League (figures 68-82) were incorporated into the "Blacks in America" exhibition illustrating various aspects of Harlem's life—the poverty, the struggle for work and education, religion, the joys of life and the indomitable spirit of Blacks. The photographers included Aaron Siskind, who had donated his personal collection of "Harlem Document" photographs to the International Museum of Photography, Beatrice Kosofsky, Jack Manning (Mendelsohn), Richard Lyon, Harold Corsini and Morris Engel.

Harlem is today the Negro metropolis and as such is everywhere known . . . So here we have Harlem—not merely a colony or a community or a settlement—not at all a "quarter" or a slum or a fringe—but a black city, located in the heart of white Manhattan, and containing more Negroes to the square mile than any other spot on earth . . .

Within the past ten years Harlem has acquired a world-wide reputation . . . It is farthest known as being exotic, colourful, and sensuous; a place of laughing, singing, and dancing; a place where life wakes up at night . . .

But, of course, no one can seriously think that the two hundred thousand and more Negroes in Harlem spend their nights on any such pleasance . . . The great bulk of them are confronted with the stern necessity of making a living, of making both ends meet, of finding money to pay the rent and keep the children fed and clothed neatly enough to attend school; their working hours are almost entirely consumed in this unromantic task . . .

There are something like one hundred and sixty coloured churches in Harlem . . . The multiplicity of churches in Harlem, and in every other Negro community, is commonly accounted for by the innate and deep religious emotion of the race . . . There is also the vital fact that coloured churches provide their members with a great deal of enjoyment aside from the joys of religion . . . The church is a stabilizing force. The integrating value of the churches in Harlem, where there are so many disintegrating forces at work, can easily be underestimated . . .

In a word, Harlem possesses in some degree all of the elements of a cosmopolitan centre . . . We find that the overwhelming majority of its people are people whose counterparts may be found in any American community. Yet as a whole community it possesses a sense of humour and a love of gaiety that are distinctly characteristic.

James Weldon Johnson *from*
Black Manhattan
(1930)

Harlem, physically, at least, has changed very little in my parents' lifetime or in mine. Now as then the buildings are old and in desperate need of repair, the streets are crowded and dirty, there are too many human beings per square block...

All of Harlem is pervaded by a sense of congestion, rather like the insistent, maddening, claustrophobic pounding in the skull that comes from trying to breathe in a very small room with all the windows shut...

James Baldwin *from "The Harlem Ghetto" in* Notes of a Native Son *(1955)*

68. Morris Engel, *(Street scene, Harlem)*, ca. 1939. Gift of Aaron Siskind*

69. Beatrice Kosofsky, *(Apartment rental sign)*, ca. 1939.
Gift of Aaron Siskind*

70. Jack Manning (Mendelsohn), *(Tenement yards)*, ca. 1939.
Gift of Aaron Siskind

71. Jack Manning (Mendelsohn), *(Inside a kitchen)*, ca. 1939.
Gift of Aaron Siskind*

72. Aaron Siskind, *(Newspaper office)*, ca. 1939.
Gift of Aaron Siskind

73. Jack Manning (Mendelsohn), *(Pickets)*, ca. 1939.
Gift of Aaron Siskind*

74. Harold Corsini, *(Job line)*, ca. 1939.
Gift of Aaron Siskind

75. Harold Corsini, *(Church service)*, ca. 1939.
Gift of Aaron Siskind*

76. Harold Corsini, *(Children in classroom)*, ca. 1939.
Gift of Aaron Siskind

77. Richard Lyon, *(Boy scout troop)*, ca. 1939.
Gift of Aaron Siskind

78. Morris Engel, *(Mother with stroller)*, ca. 1939.
Gift of Aaron Siskind

79. Jack Manning (Mendelsohn), *(Men in street)*, ca. 1939.
Gift of Aaron Siskind

80. Jack Manning (Mendelsohn), *(Woman in fur coat)*, ca. 1939.
Gift of Aaron Siskind*

81. Aaron Siskind, *(Saxophone player)*, ca. 1939.
Gift of Aaron Siskind

82. Aaron Siskind, *Savoy*, ca. 1939.
Gift of Aaron Siskind*

With the onset of World War II, a continuing migration of Blacks to the North in search of work took place. Several photographs from the 1940s and 1950s document this migration. In the 1940s Gordon Parks, noted photographer, cinematographer, poet and composer, silhouetted a man in the steam of a Pittsburgh grease plant, and a woman, with her mops and brooms, against the American flag as she cleaned an office (figures 83-84). Arthur Rothstein showed a white and a Black working together at Fort Loudon Dam in Tennessee in 1942 (figure 85).

The second World War again gave Blacks the opportunity to show their patriotism. As Dr. Martin Luther King, Jr. later wrote, "not until World War II did the Army begin to conceive that it had the right, the obligation and the ability to say that a white man in uniform must respect the dignity of a black man in uniform."[15] *A press photo issued by the U.S. Navy shows this in action, as a group of white servicemen lower a wounded black sailor to the deck (figure 86).*

Portraits of other Blacks, some famous, some not, fill out these years of change (figures 87-92). Duke Ellington playing at the Hurricane in New York City, Joe Louis defending his World Heavyweight title, Marian Anderson finally arriving on the stage of the Metropolitan Opera House, all speak to the beginnings of national recognition of achievements of Blacks.

83. Gordon Parks, *Pittsburgh Grease Plant*, March 1944.*

84. Gordon Parks, *(Cleaning woman)*, 1942.
Gift of the Library of Congress*

85. Arthur Rothstein, *Rigger and Signalman, Fort Loudon Dam, Tennessee*, 1942.
Gift of Arthur Rothstein

86. U.S. Navy, *(Wounded sailor)*, ca. 1944.
Gift of Thomas J. Maloney*

87. Clara Sipprell, *Liverpool Hazard (Ex-slave from Butler Plantation, Georgia)*, 1942.

88. Roy de Carava, *Graduation*, 1949.
Gift of Roy de Carava*

89. Gordon Parks, *Duke Ellington at the Hurricane, NYC,* April 1943.
Gift of the Library of Congress*

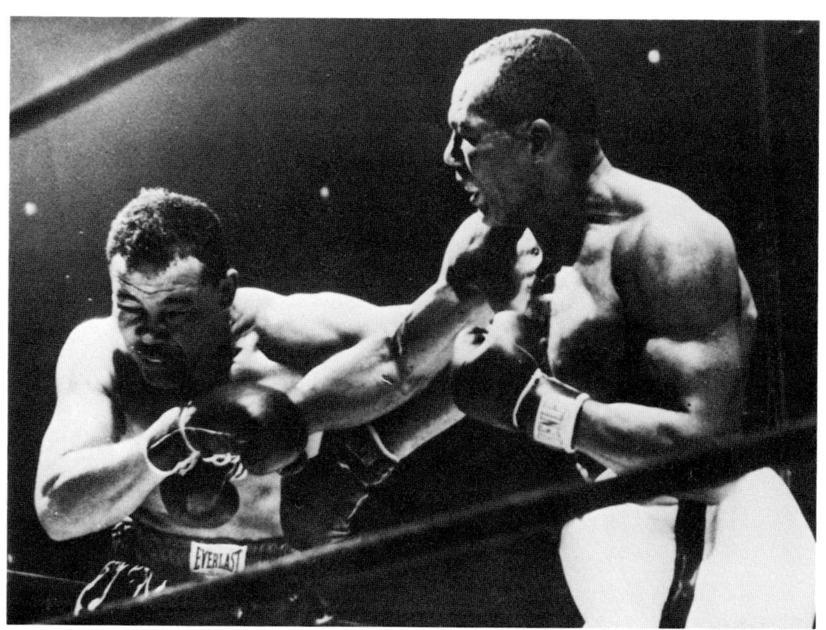

90. Associated Press, *(Joe Louis and Joe Walcott),* December 5, 1947.
Gift of Vincent S. Jones*

91. Frank Mastro (Associated Press), *(Marian Anderson on the stage of the Metropolitan Opera House),* October 7, 1954.
Gift of Vincent S. Jones*

92. Arnold Newman, *Jacob Lawrence,* 1959.
Loan from Arnold Newman

As early as 1855 Frederick Douglass wrote about being "called upon to betake myself to the Jim Crow Car.*"*[16] *Over a hundred years later, the degrading doctrines of Jim Crowism and "separate-but-equal" persisted in many parts of the country, most entrenched in the South.*

The civil rights movement exploded as legal systems forced change and resistance to change died hard. Newspapers flashed a nation glimpses of the struggle—from black children being escorted into previously all-white schools to black leaders, like Martin Luther King, Jr., being arrested, and demonstrators being doused by fire hoses to break up demonstrations to the march on Washington, D.C. in 1968 when Dr. King stood on the steps of the Lincoln Memorial and moved a nation with his words: "I have a dream that one day this nation will rise up and live out the true meaning of its creed; 'We hold these truths to be self-evident, that all men are created equal.'"[17] *(figures 93-101).*

93. Associated Press, *(Children being escorted to Little Rock School, Arkansas)*, July 25, 1957.
Gift of Vincent S. Jones*

The custom of providing separate cars for the accommodation of colored travelers, was established on nearly all the railroads of New England, a dozen years ago. Regarding this custom as fostering the spirit of caste, I made it a rule to seat myself in the cars for the accommodation of passengers generally. Thus seated, I was sure to be called upon to betake myself to the "*Jim Crow Car.*" Refusing to obey, I was often dragged out of my seat, beaten, and severely bruised, by conductors and brakemen.

Frederick Douglass *from*
My Bondage and My Freedom
(1855)

If you wish to ride with me you must come into the "Jim Crow Car"... Usually the races are mixed in there; but the white coach is all white. Of course this car is not so good as the other, but it is fairly clean and comfortable. The discomfort lies chiefly in the hearts of those four black men yonder—and in mine.

William E. B. DuBois *from*
The Souls of Black Folk
(1903)

She did not ask me what I wanted, but repeated, as though she had learned it somewhere, "We don't serve Negroes here." She did not say it with the blunt, derisive hostility to which I had grown accustomed, but, rather, with a note of apology in her voice, and fear.

James Baldwin *from*
Notes of a Native Son
(1955)

From Virginia to Florida it was a nightmare. There was no place for us to eat or sleep on the main highways. Restaurants wouldn't serve us... Some gasoline stations didn't want to sell us gas and oil. Some told us that no rest rooms were available. The looks of anger at the sight of us colored folks sitting in a nice car were frightening to see.

Mahalia Jackson *from*
Movin' On Up
(1966)

Separate-but-equal marked the last stage of the white man's flight into cultural neurosis, and the beginning of the black man's frantic striving to assert his humanity and equalize his position with the white.

Eldridge Cleaver *from*
Soul on Ice
(1968)

94. Associated Press, *(Sara and Horace Baker in their home after rock throwing wrecked their windows because they moved into a white neighborhood, Folcroft, PA)*, August 31, 1963.
Gift of Vincent S. Jones

95. Bruce Davidson, *Volunteering for "Non-Violence,"* June 1961.*

96. Bruce Davidson, *Freedom Rider,* December 1961.

97. Associated Press *(Martin Luther King, Jr., and Ralph Abernathy being arrested in Birmingham, Alabama),* April 12, 1963.
Gift of Vincent S. Jones

SOS

Calling black people
Calling all black people, man woman child
Wherever you are, calling you, urgent, come in
Black People, come in, wherever you are, urgent, calling
you, calling all black people
calling all black people, come in, black people, come on in.

Imamu Amiri Baraka *(1934–)*

In the summer of 1963 a need and a time and a circumstance and the mood of a people came together . . . the Negroes of America wrote an emancipation proclamation to themselves. They shook off three hundred years of psychological slavery and said: "We can make ourselves free."

Martin Luther King, Jr. *from*
Why We Can't Wait
(1963)

STREET DEMONSTRATION

"Hurry up Lucille or we won't get arrested with our group."
(An Eight Year Old Demonstrator, 1963)

We're hoping to be arrested
And hoping to go to jail
We'll sing and shout and pray
For Freedom and for Justice
And for Human Dignity
The fighting may be long
And some of us will die
But Liberty is costly
And ROME they say to me
Was not built in one day.

Hurry Up, Lucille, Hurry Up
We're Going to Miss Our Chance to go to Jail.

Margaret Walker *(1915–)*

98. Associated Press, *Demonstrators Doused in Alabama,* July 25, 1963. Gift of Vincent S. Jones*

99. Associated Press, *(March on Washington, D.C.),* August 28, 1963. Gift of Vincent S. Jones*

From "AN ANTE-BELLUM SERMON"

An' yo' enemies may 'sail you
In de back an' in de front'
But de Lawd is all aroun' you,
Fu' to ba' de battle's brunt.
Dey kin fo'ge yo' chains an' shackles
F'om de mountains to de sea;
But de Lawd will sen' some Moses
Fu' to set his chillun free.

Paul Laurence Dunbar *(1872-1906)*

He was The One, The Hero, The One Fearless Person for whom we had waited. I hadn't even realized before that we *had* been waiting for Martin Luther King, Jr., but we had. And I knew it for sure when my mother added his name to the list of people she prayed for every night...

He gave us back our heritage. He gave us back our homeland; the bones and dust of our ancestors, who may now sleep within our caring *and* our hearing...

He gave us continuity of place, without which community is ephemeral. He gave us home.

Alice Walker *from "Choice: A Tribute to Martin Luther King, Jr." (1973) in* In Search of Our Mothers' Gardens *(1983)*

Now is the time to make real the promises of democracy. Now is the time to rise from the dark and desolate valley of segregation to the sunlit path of racial justice. Now is the time to lift our nation from the quicksands of racial injustice to the solid rock of brotherhood. Now is the time to make justice a reality for all of God's children...

I have a dream that one day this nation will rise up and live out the true meaning of its creed; "We hold these truths to be self-evident, that all men are created equal."

Martin Luther King, Jr., *excerpts from a speech, Washington, D.C., August 28, 1963*

100. Ben Fernandez, *Martin Luther King, Jr.*, ca. 1965.
Gift of Michael Engl*

101. Associated Press, *(Coretta King and Ralph Abernathy one month after Martin Luther King, Jr.'s death)*, May 10, 1968.
Gift of Vincent S. Jones*

Photographs from the early 1970s to today, after the peak battles of the civil rights movement took place, show that life continues for Blacks—little change in some areas, great strides in others—Southern prisons still filled with Blacks, urban children whiling away their time, vast numbers of Blacks fighting in Viet Nam (figures 102-108).

The exhibition ends on a most hopeful note. It is a portrait of the Reverend Jesse Jackson campaigning for the Presidency of the United States (figure 109), bringing the exhibition full circle, from a portrait of an anonymous minister to a most famous minister reaching toward the highest honor in the country.

102. Associated Press, *(Youths rioting in East New York, Brooklyn)*, May 5, 1971.
Gift of Vincent S. Jones

103. Danny Lyon, *(Prison yard, Texas)*, 1968.

104. Associated Press, *Vanguard Arrives (Vietnam)*, June 25, 1971.
Gift of Vincent S. Jones*

105. Milton Rogovin, *(Appalachia)*, 1970
Gift of Beaumont Newhall

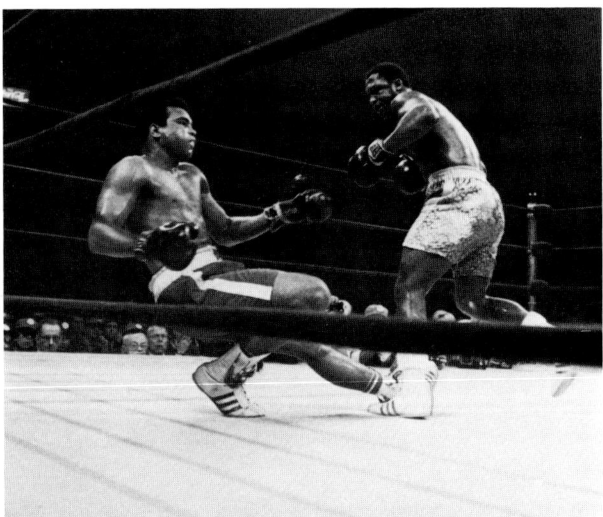

106. David Hume Kennerly *(Muhammad Ali vs. Joe Frazier)*, March 8, 1971. Gift of David Hume Kennerly

107. Associated Press, *(Pearl Bailey as American delegate to the United Nations)*, November 26, 1975.
Gift of Vincent S. Jones*

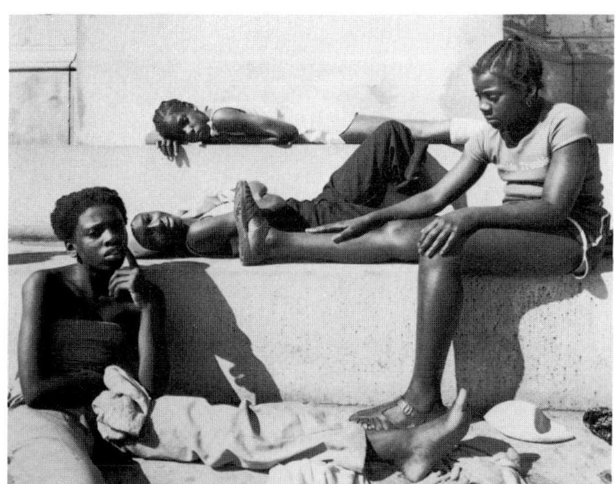

108. Nicholas Nixon, *(Urban children)*, ca. 1980*

109. Reed Hoffmann, *(Jesse Jackson campaigning in Rochester for the Presidency of the United States)*, December 16, 1983.
Gift of Gannett Rochester Newspapers*

NOTES

1. James Baldwin, *Notes of a Native Son* (Boston: Beacon Press, 1984) p. 6.
2. *Ibid.*, p. 24.
3. *Ibid.*
4. Martin Luther King, Jr., *Why We Can't Wait* (New York: Harper & Row, 1964) p. 111.
5. Frances E. W. Harper, "The Slave Auction," *The Black Poets* edited by Dudley Randall (New York: Bantam Books, 1971) p. 39.
6. Frederick Douglass, "To My Old Master, Thomas Auld," *My Bondage and My Freedom* (New York: Dover Publications, Inc., 1969) p. 426.
7. Soujourner Truth, Speech to a Convention of the American Equal Rights Association, 1867, *Black Women in White America: A Documentary History* (New York: Random House, 1973) p. 569.
8. Amanda Smith Jemand, "A Southern Woman's Appeal for Justice," *Black Women in White America*, p. 540.
9. William E. B. DuBois, *The Souls of Black Folk* reprinted in *Three Negro Classics* (New York: Avon Books, 1965) p. 239.
10. Septima P. Clark, *Echo In My Soul* (New York: E. P. Dutton & Co. 1962) p. 38.
11. Booker T. Washington, *Up From Slavery* reprinted in *Three Negro Classics* p. 106.
12. *Ibid.*, p. 168.
13. Mary Church Terrell, "What It Means to Be Colored in the Capital of the United States," (1907), *Black Women in White America*, p. 382.
14. James Weldon Johnson, *Black Manhattan* (New York: Alfred A. Knopf, 1930).
15. Martin Luther King, Jr., *loc. cit.*, p. 129.
16. Frederick Douglass, *My Bondage and My Freedom*, p. 399.
17. Martin Luther King, Jr., from a speech given in Washington, D.C., August 28, 1963, *The New York Times*, August 29, 1963.